YOU
ARE
ENOUGH

T0343747

TONY WILSON

BookPress®
publishing

Publisher's Cataloging-in-Publication Data

Names: Wilson, Tony. 1949-, author.
Title: You are enough / Tony Wilson.
Description: Second edition. | Includes bibliographical references. |
Des Moines, IA: Bookpress Publishing, 2024.
Identifiers: LCCN: 2015916839 | ISBN: 9781960259318
Subjects: LCSH Self-actualization (Psychology). | Change (Psychology). |
Success--Psychological aspects. | Self-realization. | Self-help techniques. | BISAC BODY,
MIND & SPIRIT / Inspiration & Personal Growth | SELF-HELP / Personal Growth /
Success | SELF-HELP / Personal Growth / Self-Esteem | SELF-HELP / Personal Growth /
Happiness | SELF-HELP / Self-Management / Stress Management
Classification: LCC BF637.S4 W558 2024 | DDC 158/.1--dc23

Second Edition

Printed in the United States of America
10 9 8 7 6 5 4 3 2 1

This book is dedicated to my big sister, Valdina (Punkin) Mackey, one of the richest people I knew. I began writing this at her bedside as she prepared for the transition we all make sooner or later. Her wealth rested in the relationships she developed and nurtured, and the lives she touched as she lived, what appeared to be, a simple life.

As I watched the endless stream of phone calls and visitors, each wanting to say "good-bye" and "thank you," what touched me most was the number of young people—ages four to thirty—who called her "Granny." She only had four biological grandchildren, but she was Granny to many more. That was priceless.

She showered her love and acceptance on all who came to her home. She will be missed; her spirit and courage will be long remembered. One of the last conversations we had was around the power of thought and the role thought plays in creating both one's physical, spiritual, and personal reality. In this book, I share the basis of that conversation.

This book is also dedicated to those who walk this earth feeling less than or not enough. It is my hope and belief this book will help them see the light when they are in the darkness of despair; I hope they realize there is always a healthier and easier way out.

Ockham's razor is a problem-solving principle that says, if two theories explain a phenomenon, the simplest theory is best. Not only is the information in this book simple, but it is also the easiest way to regain footing and balance in this often-confusing world.

Of all the trainings I do, the information in this book always gets a thumbs up. No matter if it's with youth, students, or parents, if it is with people in prison, business, or military, the response is always the same, "Thanks for helping me to stay Home!"

Tony Wilson

Alchemist (A helper for common people to do extraordinary things).
Here's to your awesomeness!

APPRECIATION

I offer my deep thanks to, and appreciation for, everyone who has touched my life in some way. Because of each and every one of you, I am who I am today, and this book is what it is.

Thanks to everyone who has ever been a student or participant in one of my classes or seminars. I have learned much from each of you, and because of the transformations that I have witnessed, I've been inspired to write this book and have the courage to continue on this life journey that is my passion.

I appreciate all of the many people who attended my Three Principles/ Health Realization Lunch and Learns. We all gained from the deep wisdom of Sydney Banks. It was during these lunch and learns, that I was inspired to create my Home presentation and began to truly understand the power of thought.

My appreciation goes out to all the authors that I have read and studied. Because of their deep wisdom and their determination to find the truth, I have begun to understand how life really works. It is this understanding that I am sharing in the pages of this book.

Most of all, I am grateful to you for acquiring this book. It is my hope that it will bring much love, joy, hope, peace, and appreciation to your life.

Tony Wilson

CONTENTS

1

You Are Enough

You are enough! That is one of the most important things I want you to understand and remember as you go through life. If you keep that thought in the back and front of your mind and adopt it as a foundational belief system, as a fundamental truth, your downs will be fewer, they won't be as deep, and they won't occur as often. You will also find your highs may be higher, longer lasting, and more frequent. You'll be free to use your energy for things that matter, and you won't waste as much energy on the impossible task of trying to please others or fit into a mold that was not meant for you.

I discovered the power of that statement when I met Tommy English, a 6'3", 314-pound, 60-year-old, African American male who decided he wanted more from the second part of his life than the first. Tommy spent several years in prison and left there with new skills, some helpful and some not. One thing he entered and left with was anger and a negative attitude.

I met Tommy when I served on the interview team of Project IOWA, a workplace initiative founded on the belief that everyone is entitled to dignity and respect as well as the opportunity to live the American Dream. The initiative's founders believed part of the American Dream was to have a livable wage job with benefits. Tommy came to us because he wanted the American Dream, to escape the struggle of his life. When he entered the program, his income came from doing odd jobs and delivering newspapers, which he had done for seven years.

Tommy, clad in bib overalls, was an imposing figure as he entered our small interview room. Julie Fugenschuh and I started with the routine questions we asked all participants. Midway through the interview, I noticed beads of sweat covered the entire top of his bald head. We paused the interview and attempted to put him at ease. I handed him tissues to dry his head, and we continued.

He made it through the rest of the interview with the help of a few more tissues. To his delight, we informed him we thought he was an excellent candidate for our program. This brought a light to his eyes. We informed him he needed to meet with me to identify any barriers that might interfere with him completing the program and to develop a plan to overcome those barriers. Tommy thanked us and left.

The next time I saw Tommy was at the Smokey Row Coffee shop where I held informal one-on-one meetings. He walked to the table in his customary bib overalls and sat down a little nervously. I engaged him in light conversation. As we started talking about goals and barriers to those goals, I noticed he broke into a sweat again. I paused for a moment. A quiet inner voice led me to say, "Tommy, I don't know what other people have said to you or about you in the past...or even what you say and think about yourself, but I want you to know that *you are enough* just like you are!" After I said it, I noticed drops running down his face, but they weren't coming from his bald head this time. They came from his eyes. Here was this huge bulk of a man—who served time in tough prisons—crying. Then and there, I realized the power of that statement.

Too many of us walk around with inaccurate self-assessments of who we are and what we are capable of doing. We are unaware of how our unique gifts are necessary ingredients in the soup called life. By hiding or falling short of developing our true selves, we deprive ourselves the benefit of experiencing life's joys, and we deprive others of the unique gifts we have to offer. Only when we realize *we are enough* and allow our gifts and light to shine, will we experience the peace and joy we desire.

Talking to Tommy reminded me that we are all divine beings, gifted with free will and grace. There is a distinct and powerful difference between who we *are* and what we *do*. Regardless of what we *do*, we eternally maintain our divinity. It has been said things that happen are neither good nor bad; they are only experiences that lead to desirable or undesirable results. I heard Dr. Joe Dispenza, noted researcher and lecturer in the fields of neuroscience and quantum physics, say when we view our experiences without the emotions that often accompany them—emotions that perhaps haunt us for many years—then and only then will those experiences turn to true wisdom.

You are a child of the divine, and you are worthy of the best. Once you turn your experiences into wisdom without guilt, shame, and unworthiness, you will realize and remember YOU ARE ENOUGH. You'll open the doors of possibility and allow the good things you desire and deserve to enter your life. The power is yours. Use it!

2

Don't Believe the Hype

Countless problems occur, and broken lives exist, because too many of us have believed the hype. That hype is social conditioning. It is the information we learn about ourselves and others. It is what we learned about who we are and how life works. It shapes our beliefs. These beliefs sometimes result in people settling for lives of hopelessness and unfulfilled dreams. Sadly, many of these beliefs are not true.

The hype is also those beliefs that are keeping us living small, unfulfilled lives. We are divine beings with unlimited potential, yet many of us walk around like the eagle in the story of the proverbial Eagle in the Barnyard.

In that story, an eagle was raised by chickens. Like any newborn, the eagle bonded with, and took on the characteristics of those around him. He walked around finding whatever food he could find on the ground and was content with the life he was living.

Since chickens live their lives basically earthbound, the eagle never even thought about flying, and if he did, he certainly didn't think it was possible for him since, after all, chickens don't fly! Here was this majestic being living the life of a common chicken. It was only later in life, when he found out who he really was, did he get to know the joy of soaring in the sky. All because he believed what the chickens (or society) told him about himself (the hype).

By not truly understanding who we are, we often do whatever the chickens do and tell us to do. This could be classified as living down to other's expectations. We are not chickens, and it's time to examine much of what the chickens taught us.

It is our birthright to regain our majesty. I want to help you learn to soar again to heights unimagined.

What happens when someone steps out of the social conditioning and programming that keeps him or her grounded like an eagle in the barnyard? Consider these examples:

Hype: The Earth is flat.

Truth: Christopher Columbus and others proved that was hype.

Hype: No one can run a mile under four minutes.

Truth: In 1954, Roger Bannister exposed that hype and ran the first mile in under four minutes. Forty-six days later, his record was broken. Since then, other runners lowered the record by almost 17 seconds.

Hype: If you are physically, mentally, or sexually abused, you must live as a victim.

Truth: Those in abusive situations may focus their lives on the abuse. By doing so, they may perpetuate a life of victimization. The hype says we must focus on being a victim for the rest of our lives and experience the pain of it repeatedly. That is not true. Once we learn the Hawaiian principle of "energy goes where attention flows," we can shift our focus to what we want rather than what has happened, and we can remove the emotion from the experience, turn it to wisdom, and use that wisdom to overcome challenges. We no longer have to feel pain and misery if we switch our focus from the problem to the solution.

Hype: If you are convicted of a felony, you are a felon.

Truth: The hype says what we do is what we are. When we believe the hype, we often label ourselves by what we have done. That can be confusing and detrimental to growth and development. No matter what we do, we are people, and divine ones at that. Thus, you are not a felon but a person who committed a felony.

Hype: If your family has certain genetic traits, then you too will exhibit those traits.

Truth: Much of Bruce Lipton[1] and other scientists' work shows genetics indicate only a tendency toward certain behaviors or conditions. Your environment determines whether those traits manifest. That environment is created and controlled by how we think and feel. Thoughts can elevate emotions. Those emotions foster chemical reactions in the body, which determine the manifestation of those genetic tendencies. In other words, we have more control of our destiny than we think, but only if we don't believe the hype.

Take a moment to examine more examples of hype. Do you know someone or something that proves these untrue? If so, write a true statement.

Hype: Single mothers are not capable of successfully raising boys.

Truth: _____

_____

_____

_____

Hype: Girls are not as good as boys in math and science.

Truth: _____

_____

_____

_____

Hype: If you have terminal cancer, you will die soon.

Truth: _____

_____

_____

_____

Hype: If you are not raised in an enriching environment as a child, you are doomed to failure.

Truth: _____

_____

_____

_____

Can you think of more? If so, write them below.

Hype: _____

_____

_____

Truth: _____

_____

_____

_____

Hype: _____

_____

_____

Truth: _____

_____

_____

_____

Hype: _____

_____

_____

Truth: _____

      _____

      _____

      _____

Hype: _____

      _____

      _____

Truth: _____

      _____

      _____

      _____

Hype: _____

      _____

      _____

Truth: _____

      _____

      _____

      _____

These beliefs have one thing in common: They are merely beliefs, which are not always truths. We innocently pick up beliefs everywhere. We even make some up. As is often said, "Beliefs are just thoughts we keep thinking over and over again." We can have a belief about anything we choose. All we must do is think about it long enough; and then it becomes a belief.

That is both the good and bad news. If the beliefs we have

are helpful and bring us good feelings, we can keep them. If the belief isn't helpful or doesn't bring good feelings, it is worth a closer look.

What is some of the hype you believe or believed about yourself? List those, then write a truth below.

Hype: _____

_____

_____

Truth: _____

_____

_____

_____

Hype: _____

_____

_____

Truth: _____

_____

_____

_____

Hype: _____

_____

_____

Truth: _____

_____

_____

_____

Hype: _____

_____

_____

Truth: _____

_____

_____

_____

Hype: _____

_____

_____

Truth: _____

_____

_____

_____

As you continue in this book, we will look at beliefs and the thoughts that create them. Hopefully, you'll realize some unhelpful and self-limiting beliefs that need close scrutiny and healthy modification.

3

The Power of Thought

This book is about thought and the power it possesses. Albert Einstein said, "We cannot solve our problems with the same thinking we used when we created them." Many of us live our lives as if we are hopeless, helpless, and powerless. We might feel this way because of social conditioning. Unfortunately, this crippling conditioning often innocently comes from those we turn to for the hope, the help, and the power we need.

According to Bruce Lipton in *Biology of Belief*[1], much of this conditioning comes early in life. He says in our first six years, we essentially download everything we see, hear, and feel into our subconscious minds. Our parents innocently feed us much of this information—accurate or not—because they too learned to believe the hype. This information and conditioning also come from schools, peers, the media, and religious institutions. Much of this social conditioning cripples us, turning us into beggars, and we end up suffering and lacking the awareness of the awesome power we possess. As a result, we beg for scraps when it is our birthright to settle for nothing but the best.

How do we reclaim our birthright? The process is simple and common sense. It is the initial step of healing and reclamation. However, we know common sense isn't always common practice. Many theories talk about how to live a fuller, richer, more purposeful life. Instead of just talking about it, this book presents a simple, practical way to attain, retain, and maintain such a life.

The simple fact is that you have tremendous power within you, and your Creator endowed this power upon you. This is the power to be, do, and have everything your heart desires. Ancient and spiritual texts proclaim this truth. Christian literature states, "...seek, and ye shall find; knock, and the door shall be opened unto you...ask, and it shall be given you." It also says, "You have not because you ask not." In other ancient texts, we are told to look within for answers. Christians are even told by Jesus that He would leave us the "Comforter" to provide for our every "comfort." This Comforter lies within us. The message is always the same. Let's see how "the Word" (thought) can help take us back *Home*.

4

There's No Place Like Home

In this book, *Home* is a state of mind, experienced as love, passion, happiness, optimism, hopefulness, and contentment. This state is our birthright. We can liken this return *Home* to the parable of the Prodigal Son's return home. He was welcomed by his father and experienced the peace, joy, happiness, and love of returning *Home*.

Have you experienced a similar journey or challenge where you got lost and were given grace when you returned *Home*? One might note these journeys and challenges are part of life's adventure, and like the Prodigal Son—who asked for his inheritance while his father was still alive, squandered it on wild living, and then returned home a beggar—no forgiveness was needed because the father never judged the son in the first place; he only gave him the wonderful gift of grace.

We can ease tremendous burdens by knowing that one of

the Spirit's gifts is free will. It is an invitation to adventure and growth, as in Joseph Campbell's hero's journey,[2] where the hero is prone to falling into the abyss of misery, pain, and unhappiness before again returning *Home*. That is all part of our learning and often the point at which we reclaim our power.

Fortunately, the gift that accompanies free will is grace. Grace prevents us from spending too much time beating ourselves up when we find ourselves in the abyss and helps us escape it with free will. It also prevents us from unnecessarily beating up others as well.

If you are tired of living this way, it's time to begin the journey back to wholeness.

5

The Journey Back
to Wholeness

We can learn a lot from the wisdom of movies. Many of us are like Simba in *The Lion King*[3] when his father, Mufasa, told him, "You have forgotten who you are!" We often forget who we are and the great power we possess.

To get a proper understanding of who we truly are, take a look at a healthy newborn baby. Once a newborn is dry, fed, and has had a nap, the baby instinctively becomes content, peaceful, calm, satisfied, secure, and happy. No instructions needed; no classes to attend. This is how we are hardwired from the start. Since this is typical with healthy newborns, this must be our default state prior to social conditioning. It is only when we forget who we are and get caught up in the hype that we abandon the calm and contentment we desire.

Also, consider Dorothy from *The Wizard of Oz*. After all the obstacles she and her friends faced, she realized, "There's no place like *home*." She also discovered she always had the power within her. She just needed to realize it. When I use the word *Home*, I am not discussing a house because, unfortunately, unpleasant things often happen in and around houses. Instead, I'm discussing our psychological *Home*, our natural state of being.

When we forget that we are "children of the divine" and begin to focus on thoughts, feelings, behaviors, and what other people say and do, we often leave our happy *Homes* and find ourselves on what I call the *Porch*. When we are on the *Porch*, we may begin to feel bored, pessimistic, frustrated, overwhelmed, disappointed, and doubtful.

And from time to time, we may find ourselves even further from *Home* and end up in the *Yard*. The *Yard* is another state of mind characterized by negative emotions such as worry, blame, discouragement, anger, and stress. Some of us find ourselves in the *Yard* far too often.

Those who continue focusing on conditions or things that other people do and say (things almost always out of their control), often find themselves in the *Neighborhood*. This state of mind, far from our default setting (*Home*), is characterized by revenge, hatred, rage, and jealousy. The crime and violence that take place usually happen when a person is in a *Neighborhood* state of mind.

Every once in a while, we hear of someone so far from *Home* that they need a *Passport* to get back *Home*. They are often referred to as "mentally ill" and may require time to regain a healthy state of mind (see Figure 1).

Home	Porch	Yard	Neighborhood	Passport
Love	Bored	Worry	Anger	Fear
Happiness	Impatient	Discour-agement	Hatred	Despair
Optimism	Overwhelmed		Rage	Depression
Hopefulness	Disappointed		Jealousy	Powerlessness
Contentment	Doubt			

Figure 1

The good news is these states of mind are temporary. In time, we can return *Home*, and we stay there until our thoughts betray us again. Everyone, even the most troubled people, return *Home* from time to time. The returns may be brief or infrequent, but they do happen.

How do we allow ourselves to fall into unhealthy states like the *Porch*, *Yard*, and *Neighborhood*? Beyond social conditioning, it is often caused by ignorance and innocence. Ignorance occurs because no one explained how life works... that it is always our thinking that leads us innocently away from *Home*. Once we understand how we create our realities with our thoughts, we can seize control of our lives and create new, more desirable ones.

I want to help you regain control of your life and become more intentional about the life you create. To do that, let me explain the process of creating your reality on a moment-to-moment basis. See Figure 2.

Fact #1:   Everything begins with a **thought**.

Fact #2:   Thoughts release **chemicals** into our bloodstream.

Fact #3:   Chemicals create **feelings**.

Fact #4:   Feelings influence our **actions**.

Fact #5:   Our actions result in **consequences/reality**.

Thoughts • Chemicals • Feelings • Actions • Consequences

Figure 2

We follow this process moment-to-moment, hour-by-hour, day-by-day to create our realities. We are free to stop this chain of events at any time up to and including the action phase. If we don't like a thought, we are free to choose a different thought that is more suitable to our values and goals.

Don't worry about running out of thoughts because, according to Bruce Lipton in *The Biology of Belief*[1], we have between 60,000 and 70,000 thoughts a day. He goes on to say 90 percent of those thoughts are the same thoughts we had the day before. What's even worse, he says 75 percent of those thoughts are negative. Since we are often creatures of habit, does that make us negative creatures of habit?

Lipton goes on to say, when we think negative thoughts, we secrete stress hormones into our blood stream. This starts a negative spiral because these hormones produce negative feelings. When we feel bad, we tend to behave in a less-than-optimal manner. This behavior usually brings negative consequences, causing us to create more negative thoughts and negative hormones, and the cycle repeats. Over time, if the negative spiral continues, we have a negative temperament, and ultimately, a negative personality.

As stated earlier, we might have been innocent and ignorant of how and why we feel the way we feel and why we do the things we do. Knowing this process of a negative spiral can help us seize control of our lives and personal realities. We are in charge of our lives and how we respond to them.

Here's an example of how this "thoughts–chemical–feelings–actions–consequences" process works. Picture sitting at a stoplight on a bright, sunny day. Your favorite music is playing, and you are at *Home*, feeling secure, content, happy, peaceful, and calm. Just as the light turns green, a car comes flying through the intersection, barely missing you. As if you are on autopilot, your first thought might be, "That jerk!" You start feeling angry, then you cuss, make hand gestures, and maybe chase them down the street (actions). Before you know it, you find yourself in the *Neighborhood* (consequence).

All because of that jerk, right? Not so fast. Did the jerk cause your thoughts, chemicals, feelings, actions, and consequences (ending up in the *Neighborhood*)? Let's rewind and try this again.

You are at the same intersection, the same red light, the same music is playing, and you have the same *Home* feeling. Everything is the same. Again, as the light turns green, a car flies through the intersection, barely missing you. This time you get a glimpse of the driver and see it is your neighbor, Mrs. Johnson, and her baby in a car seat in back. You know her baby has asthma and sometimes needs to be rushed to the hospital for emergency treatment. You notice her baby is flailing around in the car seat. Your first thought is, "I hope she is all right," and you feel compassion for them. You follow (action) Mrs. Johnson to the hospital to see if you can help. Afterward, you may notice you may still be at *Home* rather than in the *Neighborhood* like you were in the first scenario!

Why did you end up in the *Neighborhood* in the first scenario and still at *Home* in the second?

Following the thought–chemical–feeling–action–consequence sequence, you discover it wasn't that jerk who caused you to leave *Home* and end up in the *Neighborhood*. It was your thoughts about that supposed jerk, which caused your feelings and actions. By contrast, when you saw the baby and Mrs. Johnson, your compassion took over. You felt compassion, you acted compassionately by following her to the hospital, and you managed to keep yourself safely at *Home*.

Whenever we find ourselves away from *Home*, it is because our belief system has kicked in. Your belief system is the cause of the thought, chemicals, feelings, actions, and resulting consequences.

A belief system is a series of thoughts we repeatedly think. When we think the same things, we create habits. Once our thoughts become habits, our subconscious minds take over, and our bodies go on autopilot. That's how we become creatures of habit. That's why 90 percent of the thoughts we have are the same thoughts we had the day before. And that is why our lives look the same as they did the day before.

Our belief systems are like tapes playing unnoticed in our

subconscious minds. One of those tapes could be labeled "that jerk." When a so-called jerk shows up, the thoughts and feelings contained within that belief system are triggered.

At the intersection, you were hijacked by your belief system. As soon as the car ran the red light, you felt angry (feeling), maybe you automatically started cussing, making hand gestures, and chasing them (actions). Does it make you wonder how many other times you are hijacked by your belief system?

Many times, we are hijacked because our egos get involved. When that happens, insecurity kicks in, and we go into fight or flight mode. Before we know it, we find ourselves in the *Yard*! Use the practice exercise below to examine the things that drive you into the yard.

A. List three things that drive you into the *Yard*.

1._____

2._____

3._____

What is the belief system behind each? For example, if we get upset when someone cuts in front of us in a long line, our belief system might be:

1. People should wait their turns.

2. People who cut in line are rude.

3. Rude people don't deserve respect.

4. Rude people deserve to be chastised.

Therefore, we may feel justified in reacting negatively toward the person.

B. What is the belief system behind each item in part A?

1._____

_____

2._____

_____

3._____

_____

How did it feel writing the statements in part A? Did just thinking about those stir anger? If so, that's why it's important to be mindful of our thoughts and choose them carefully. We must pay attention to our feelings; they are good indications of the quality of our thinking. If something doesn't feel right, we have a chance to stop and wait for a better thought. We can also examine our belief systems and discard unhealthy or unhelpful ones to improve the quality of our lives.

6

Outlaw Words

Outlaw words are words that can automatically cause discomfort. For me, one of those outlaw words is "should." The word "should" carries judgment and can evokes feelings of resentment, guilt, blame, or shame when talking about ourselves or others. Changing "should" to "could" releases judgment and guilt and, instead, offers us a choice. Saying "I should get up and exercise" might cause a feeling of guilt if we decide to stay in bed. However, saying, "I could get up and exercise" lets us know we have a choice. It doesn't carry the accompanying guilt that "should" produces. Many of us *should* all over ourselves and others far too often.

Another outlaw word is *try*. My hero from *Star Wars* is Yoda. He is famous for one of his admonitions to Luke Skywalker: "Do or do not. There is no 'try.'" The word "try" robs our intentions of their power. It gives us an easy out, an excuse to quit. By only trying, we feel justified saying, "At least, I tried!" It is more effective to firmly set our intentions and to use our awesome power to focus on those intentions.

Words like "kinda" and "just" can also diminish the statements they modify. If a person says, "I kinda like you," then we may wonder, "Do you like me or not?" Or someone says, "I am just a teacher," then we may ask, "Is that a good thing or a bad thing?" We don't want to minimize the people, things, or accomplishments that are important to us.

7

Mind-Body Connection

In the movie *The Secret*, it is stated that "thoughts become things." By simply having a thought, we cause our brains to produce a chemical (thing) that impacts our emotions and our bodies. This means there is no such thing as an idle thought. Every thought that we focus on impacts our mental and physical well-being. That also means we can use thoughts as weapons or as tools. By thoughts alone, we can create stress hormones that weaken our bodies (weapon) or create positive hormones (tools) to create more positive personal realities.

While we think distressful thoughts, feel distressful feelings, and do distressful things, the stress hormones intended for fight or flight (and not day-to-day living) pump into our systems. During fight or flight, our brains send most of our blood to our arms and legs, so we can flee the threat. The other body systems slow down to conserve energy. Most non-essential systems shut down. One of those is the immune system. Stressful times make our bodies susceptible to disease. The more stress we experience and create, the more stress hormones we release, and the more prone we are to getting sick.

Thankfully, the same is true for healthy thoughts, feelings, and actions. The more we experience those, the more supportive hormones we release, and the better we feel and operate. As you can see, we have more control over our mental and physical health than we may have known.

8

Amygdala Hijacking

According to Daniel Goleman, in *Working with Emotional Intelligence*[4], we often have our thoughts hijacked by our amygdala, one of the oldest parts of the brain. Goleman goes on to say one of its functions is storing memories of emotional events. It also plays a role in emotional reactions. Because it is one of the oldest parts of the brain, it plays a critical role in keeping us safe.

Goleman says it also has a decision-making role. If the brain receives a signal of a perceived attack, then there is a sudden reaction. If similar life or death situations are stored in the brain as memories, we are in danger of an amygdala hijacking. The reasoning part of the brain is bypassed, and the situation instead generates an instant response. This response served our ancestors well when they were in danger of being eaten alive or being attacked by nearby rivals. Today, no saber-toothed tigers prowl our neighborhoods, and for most people, the chance of a violent attack by neighbors is unlikely.

That being said, if you've experienced trauma (and we all have), our amygdala may have stored those as memories and could evoke violent and instantaneous hijackings. This is similar to what happens to those who suffer from PTSD. Our perceptions and belief systems—more so than actual danger—cause most modern-day amygdala hijackings. If we can catch ourselves at the early feeling stage, we can reframe thoughts before we commit an action we might regret later.

9

Belief Systems

Many, if not all, negative emotions are the result of our belief systems and emotional memories. Seldom are negative emotions the result of what's happening now. Social conditioning, emotional memories, subconscious belief systems, and/or a combination of these nearly always cause our negative emotions. Consider these scenarios:

- A constant banging noise irritates you. Is your irritation caused by the noise or by your beliefs and thoughts about the banging? I argue that it is your thoughts and beliefs in the context. Why? You likely wouldn't be irritated by the banging if you were trapped under rubble, and the banging sound came from the shovels of your rescuers.

- A dog constantly barking nearby angers you. Is this

caused by the barking dog? No, I say your thoughts and belief system about the barking dog that caused the anger. In another context, you probably would not be angry if you were lost, and the barking dogs were bloodhounds leading a search party looking for you.

• The trash in your neighborhood upsets you. Are you upset because of the trash? I say no. If you were temporarily blinded and the first thing you saw once your vision returned was trash on the ground, you would probably be happy to see anything at all!

• Your children leave muddy footprints on the carpet, muddy clothes on the furniture, empty plates and glasses on the table, and they're sound asleep on the couch. Would you yell at them? Probably not, especially if they had been lost for four days and they finally found their way home, hungry and tired.

The context changes your thoughts. You seldom, if ever, leave *Home* because of what is happening now. It is almost always because of a thought based on your belief system, a memory, your social conditioning, or fear of what might happen in the future.

List three things that take you into the *Yard*, then reframe each to one in a way that will keep you safely at *Home*.

Some things that usually take me out into the *Yard* are:

1._____

_____

_____

2._____

_____

_____

3._____

_____

_____

Here's how I can reframe those to remove the emotional charge:

1._____

_____

_____

2._____

_____

_____

3._____

_____

_____

Hopefully by now, you realize it's not what happens to you that causes your feelings and actions; it's how you *think* about what happens to you that causes them. It all begins with thoughts, and guess who the thinkers is? YOU!

Knowing this, you have the opportunity to step out of the victim roles and think in ways that benefit you, so you can feel the way you want to feel and do what brings you joy.

10

Our Master's Degree

We are endowed with many gifts as our birthrights such as free will, feelings, and choices. We were even given an advanced degree, a Master's Degree or an M.S.U.: a Master's in *M*aking *S*tuff *U*p. We use this degree continuously. Some of the stuff we make up is beneficial to our well-being; some is not.

If we are cut off in traffic, we could use our M.S.U. to decide whoever cut us off is a jerk. We could get angry, yell and scream, and pump those stress hormones into our blood stream, or we can use our M.S.U. to be grateful that we avoided the accident. We can choose to pump those positive hormones into our blood stream and feel gratitude and a sense of well-being instead.

The good news is we can always choose how we think about the world and the people in it. When we accept the fact that through our thinking we create our realities, then we can be more purposeful in creating the lives we want. Once we determine how we want to live our lives—peacefully, joyously, contently—then we can focus our thoughts on the things that lead us to feel that way. If we want to live our lives as peacefully as possible, then we can tell ourselves in any situation, "I can choose peace, or I can choose other than peace." The choice is always ours. Choose wisely!

11

The Gift of Forgiveness

Most of us struggle to stay at *Home* at times. Much of what causes us to stray from *Home* is traced back to unforgiveness. The quickest way back *Home* in any situation is to forgive. When asked if they have forgiven someone for something unforgivable, most people say "yes." When asked about how they felt after they forgave, they say words like "relief," "liberation," "freedom," and "unburdened." As the saying goes, "Forgiveness is not something you give to someone else; it is a gift you give to yourself." When we forgive someone, it's helpful to remember we forgive the person, not necessarily the actions. We all do things we regret, and we all deserve forgiveness.

This forgiveness could begin with forgiving ourselves. We often carry guilt, shame, and fear from the past. This is *our junk in our trunk.* Our beliefs that we have sinned often generate these feelings. The word "sin" is an archery term, and it means we missed the mark. We all miss the mark from time to time. Thankfully, we are granted grace, so we can correct our sins. We can adjust our aim, and move on with a spirit of love, peace, and joy.

For those who refuse to forgive both ourselves and others, consider this popular saying: "Unforgiveness is like drinking poison and hoping the other person dies." All the while, the poison of unforgiveness eats us up inside. The poison is the stress-related chemicals we pump into our blood stream every time we think about that person or situation. The poison could be resentment, anger, frustration, guilt, or shame. It all eats us up inside, and it is all unnecessary, unhealthy, and unhelpful.

The poison of unforgiveness reminds me of the story of the two monks:[5]

"Two monks were making a pilgrimage to venerate the relics of a great Saint. During the course of their journey, they came to a river where they met a beautiful young woman—an apparently worldly creature, dressed in expensive finery and with her hair done up in the latest fashion. She was afraid of the current and afraid of ruining her lovely clothing, so she asked the brothers if they might carry her across the river.

"The younger and more exacting of the brothers was offended at the very idea and turned away with an attitude of disgust. The older brother didn't hesitate, and quickly picked the woman up on his shoulders, carried her across the river,

and set her down on the other side. She thanked him and went on her way, and the brother waded back through the waters.

*"The monks resumed their walk, the older one in perfect equanimity and enjoying the beautiful countryside, while the younger one grew more and more brooding and distracted, so much so that he could keep his silence no longer and suddenly burst out, 'Brother, we are taught to avoid contact with women, and there you were, not just touching a woman, but **carrying her on your shoulders!**'*

"The older monk looked at the younger with a loving, pitiful smile and said, 'Brother, I set her down on the other side of the river; you are still carrying her.'"

What are you still carrying? It may be time to put some stuff down.

Think of five things you carry with you from the past that you have not forgiven someone, or yourself, for. List them below. How many are worth carrying into the future? Lighten your load by forgiving as many as you can.

1. _____

   _____

2. _____

   _____

3. _____

   _____

4._____

_____

5._____

_____

12

Ain't Nothing Wrong With You!

I contend that, except for a miniscule percentage of people, there is absolutely nothing wrong with us or almost anybody we know. Most of us function perfectly. Based on our thoughts, the quality and quantity of chemicals flowing through our systems makes our physical equipment respond as it is designed to do. If any of us has behavioral issues, little to nothing is wrong with us. If we feel lonely, nothing is wrong with us. If someone is in prison for theft, nothing is wrong with that person. If we are addicted to drugs, nothing is wrong with us.

Take these scenarios:

• Larry is in some type of detention because he keeps getting in trouble. There's nothing wrong with Larry. His mental apparatus works perfectly. Remember the thought–chemical–feeling–action–consequence process? Larry may have been desperate and thought he needed or wanted things in other people's houses. Based on that thought, he felt if he took those things, he would be happy. So, he acted on the thoughts and feelings, got caught, and wound up detained (consequences). His mental apparatus worked like most everyone else's. He went through the same thought process we all do. The problem was not in the thought process; it was in the content of the thoughts. If we all thought like this, we might all act the same way. Like Sting says in his song *Tomorrow We'll See*, "Don't judge me. You could be me in another life, in another set of circumstances."

• Bill was mentally abused and abandoned as a child. His belief system tells him he is unworthy, unwanted, and unlovable. He does not like or trust people because of this past trauma. When someone cuts in front of him in line, he thinks the person did it because he knows how unworthy Bill is. Bill gets angry (emotional hijacking), yells and pushes the line-cutter, and is arrested for assault. Once again, the thought process worked as it was designed to work. The content of Bill's thought and belief system were the problems. There is nothing wrong with Bill.

Hope resides in these examples. It is easier to change

thoughts than it is to change behavior. Behavior is step four in the process. It is the result of thoughts, chemicals, and feelings. If we can change our thoughts and know that we are enough, that we are worthy of dignity and respect, that we are divine beings, then our chemicals, feelings, and actions change automatically.

It's time to stop punishing people for behavior and start educating them about thought and the role it plays in creating reality. That is a much better, cheaper, and more effective alternative.

13

Alignment

One key to a happier, more fulfilling life is to know when we are in and out of alignment. We might ask, "Alignment with what?" Esther Hicks[6] teaches us alignment is with our Higher Power or Source (Love). When we are in alignment, we feel love, joy, passion, positive, optimistic, hopeful, and content, just like being at *Home*. Hicks says we have an "internal guidance system" that lets us know when we are in and out of alignment. When we are aware of this "internal guidance system," we can more easily make the necessary adjustments that keep us closer to *Home*, and we can do it more often.

She goes on to say this "internal guidance system" is composed of our feelings. If we notice how we feel when we do and say things, we can tell if we are in or out of alignment. When we feel good, we are most likely in alignment with our true selves. If the things we do or think don't feel good, it's time to do and think something else. That may mean leaving a job or relationship that is unfulfilling (out of alignment). We can also change the way we look at or think about our jobs or relationships. When we are out of alignment, we can also change the way we look at or think about ourselves. Or we can bring ourselves back into alignment by changing the way we look at, think about, or treat others.

Once again, the power is in our hands. We don't need to worry and create more negative thoughts or feelings when we are not where we want to be. Hicks states "the best way to know what you want is to know what you don't want." Use that information to refocus and move toward a new goal.

Try it. Fill in the worksheet on the next page. (Used with permission from Natalie Ledwell's *Ultimate Success Master Class*[7]). See how clearly you know what you want once you know what you don't want.

Directions: First, fill in column one with things you don't want. Next, look at the things you don't want and change them to something you do want. Write those things in column two. The first is done for you.

Things I Don't Want	Things I Do Want
1. I don't want to feel bad about myself.	1. I do want to see the best in myself at all times.
2.	2.
3.	3.
4.	4.
5.	5.
6.	6.
7.	7.
8.	8.
9.	9.
10.	10.
11.	11.
12.	12.

Now that you know what you want, focus your attention on those things. Once you do that, more of those things enter your reality. Attaining and maintaining alignment is an on-going process. The keys are being present and mindful; after that, the next step will be clear. Live life one step at a time in alignment, and the journey can be most enjoyable.

14

Living Unconditional Lives

Esther Hicks[6] also talks about living "unconditional lives." Many of us are familiar with unconditional love. When we have unconditional love for somebody, we love them regardless of what they do or say. Living unconditional lives means we decide on how we want to live and then live that way regardless of the conditions around us. Some may think this is impossible, or difficult at best. Impossible, no. Difficult, maybe. With our thoughts and our belief systems, we give meaning to everything around us. When we are able to remove the emotions from anything, then we can access the deep well of wisdom within all of us. If we realize "it-is-what-it-is," then we're able to avoid much of the drama that we create in our lives.

A. Choose the ideal emotional state of mind—joy, peace, happiness, or any emotional state—that you'd like to live in unconditionally, and write it on the line below.

Ideal Emotional State: _____

B. Work to remain in that emotional state, predominantly, for the next hour. After an hour, come back and answer these questions.

    1. Were you able to remain, predominantly, in your ideal emotional state? _____

    2. Were you able to remain in that state regardless of triggers that usually drive you to the porch or the yard? _____

    3. If yes, why were you able to remain in your ideal state this time? _____

    4. What was the impact of remaining in that state?

        _____

        _____

        _____

    5. Was it worth the effort? _____

    6. If you were not able to stay in that state, why not?

        _____

        _____

        _____

C. Work to remain in that emotional state, predominantly, for the next 24 hours. After 24 hours, come back and answer the questions below.

1. Were you able to remain, predominantly, in your ideal emotional state? _____

2. Were you able to remain in that state regardless of triggers that usually drive you to the porch or the yard? _____

3. If yes, why were you able to remain in your ideal state this time? _____

4. What was the impact of remaining in that state?

   _____

   _____

   _____

5. Was it worth the effort? _____

6. If you were not able to stay in that state, why not?

   _____

   _____

   _____

Could you do it for a week? Give it a whirl, then come back and answer the questions again.

1. Were you able to remain, predominantly, in your ideal emotional state? _____

2. Were you able to remain in that state regardless of triggers that usually drive you to the porch or the yard? _____

3. If yes, why were you able to remain in your ideal state this time? _____

4. What was the impact of remaining in that state?

   _____

   _____

   _____

5. Was it worth the effort? _____

6. If you were not able to stay in that state, why not?

   _____

   _____

   _____

Many people who do this exercise find that once they set an intention to live a certain way, not only are they able to do it, but desirable things seem to flow into their lives, often giving them more of what they wanted. Esther Hicks defines the law of attraction as "the essence of that which is like unto itself is drawn."[6] Live in a state of joy, and more things to be joyful about will enter your life. Live in a state of pessimism, and more pessimism is drawn to you. What you focus on grows. Once again, it is clear we have much more control of our lives than we think. Take advantage of your power, and stay out of the *Grave Robber's Club*.

15

The Grave Robber's Club

Are you a member of the Grave Robber's Club? Not sure? Let me explain.

To start, we must realize and believe that everything in the past is dead and buried, and it will stay dead and buried as long as we don't think about it. As soon as we think about it, it's like going to a grave, digging up the past, dragging it to the present, performing mouth-to-mouth resuscitation on it, and bringing the past back to life. When we do that, we have the same thoughts and feelings we had in the past (and pump the same chemicals into our blood system that we pumped into it in the past). We are essentially re-living the past by thought alone. We can tell if we're in the *Grave Robber's Club* if we dwell in, and continually relive, the past day after day. If this sounds familiar, maybe it's time to get out of that club. The good news is we can get out whenever we choose.

A pattern of how we feel and how we act emerges here. It is based on the thoughts on which we choose to focus. All we have to remember is DNR or Do Not Resuscitate. Let the past stay buried! It's not always easy especially when we're regularly exposed to the same people or situations. Change is gradual, and it begins when we choose how we look at and think about things.

Some of us may feel trapped in a situation; however, Eckhart Tolle in *A New Earth*[8] reminds us we have three choices in any situation. One, we can accept the situation and move on. Two, we can change ourselves or the situations. (We know how difficult it is to change someone else, so the change must be within us.) Three, we can leave. We're never stuck because one of those choices helps us decide what to do. A decision is a choice. We always have a choice.

What do we do with pleasant memories from the past, the ones we want to keep and the ones that make us feel good. Hold on to them if they feel good. It means we are in alignment and not in the *Grave Robber's Club*. We're on Memory Lane. Cherish those thoughts. They not only feel good, but those thoughts bathe our bodies with those positive hormones. Better feelings lead to better actions. Those actions bring better results!

On the lines below, list five things from the past that take you out to the yard and beyond every time you think about them:

1._____

_____

_____

2._____

_____

_____

3._____

_____

_____

4._____

_____

_____

5._____

_____

_____

Is it worth thinking the same old thoughts, feeling the same old feelings, and pumping those same old chemicals into your system? If so, pump on. If not, forgive those things and people. Cross out the ones you no longer want to revisit and carry with you, then move on with new thoughts, new feelings, new actions, and a new life.

16

Conclusion

We have more control over our lives than we ever imagined, and through the power of thought, we can create and control our mental and physical realities. We can decide how we want to feel and how we want to live. We can take control of the thoughts to focus on. We can pay close attention to how we feel because our feelings are good indicators of the quality of our thoughts. We can forgive often, do as Joseph Campbell suggested and "follow your bliss," and most of all, *WE CAN KEEP OUR BUTTS AT HOME!*

In case you read this book and have those pesky "yeah, buts," ("Yeah, that sounds good, but...") drop me a line and share your thoughts: tony.wilson58@gmail.com

References

1. Lipton, B. (2008). *The biology of belief.* New York, NY: Hay House.

2. Campbell, J. (2008). *The Hero with a Thousand Faces.* Novato, CA: New World Library.

3. McArthur, S. (Executive producer), Schmacher, T. (Executive producer), Hahn, D. (Producer), Dewey, A. (Associate producer), Minkoff, R. (Director), Allen, R. (Director). *The Lion King* (Motion picture), 1995, USA: Walt Disney Home Video.

4. Goleman, D. (1998). *Working with Emotional Intelligence.* New York, NY: Bantam Books.

5. The story of the two monks. *Fish eaters.* Retrieved from https://www.fisheaters.com/twomonks.html

6. Hicks, E., & Hicks, J. (2009). *The vortex: Where the law of attraction assembles all cooperative relationships.* New York, NY: Hay House.

7. Ledwell, N. (2015). *Ultimate Success Master Class.* Retrieved from www.ultimatesuccessmasterclass.com. For more information visit: bit.ly/1NTzsd7

8. Tolle, E. (2008). *A New Earth: Awakening to your life's purpose.* New York, NY: Penguin Group.